DECLARING
YOUR
WORTH

DECLARING
YOUR
WORTH

How to Receive Your
Heavenly Inheritance

Craig A. Miller

Author of
When Your Mate Is Emotionally Unavailable

YorkshirePublishing
www.yorkshirepublishing.com
Write Now.

ISBN: 978-1-942451-78-5
Declaring Your Worth
Reprint Copyright © 2017 by Craig A Miller

For permission requests, write to the publisher at the address below.

Yorkshire Publishing
3207 South Norwood Avenue
Tulsa, Oklahoma 74135
www.YorkshirePublishing.com
918.394.2665

Table of Contents

Your Worth

When I was at the home of a friend named Todd, I asked him to show me one of his woodworking projects that was almost finished. When I shared my honest thoughts of how impressed I was with his craftsmanship, Todd immediately held the piece of handcrafted work higher in the air to point out some of the flaws in his project. His response took me by surprise and gave me the impression his own talent was not good enough to be accepted. As I drove home that day, I realized even though it was obvious to me how talented Todd appeared to be, *he* was not able to believe in himself and his own abilities.

If you have ever believed what you say, think, or feel is *not good enough*, you are not alone. As a counselor for over thirty years, I have found the struggle to believe in yourself and the questioning of your abilities has been, without hesitation, among the most destructive and the most common underlying negative issue that radically affects how you think about yourself and subsequently respond to life situations.

Your Worth Comes from How You Are Treated

Questioning or doubting your abilities is actually a result of deeper issues that originate from a lack of self-worth. Without going into too much detail, your self-worth primarily originates from how you are treated by the important people in your life. In essence, the amount of loving affection, words of encouragement, and positive events you encounter in your child and teenage years will greatly determine the measurement of worth and value you believe about yourself. How you are treated by others later in life can also affect your opinion about yourself, but your positive or negative belief system primarily begins earlier in life. For example, if your caregivers showed an interest in you by giving words of encouragement about something you accomplished, their interest would create a belief that your activity is worthwhile. And if your activity is worthwhile, then you will believe you are worthwhile. Conversely, a lack of affection and little interest in your activities will create a belief there is little about you that is worthy. When your sense of worth is low, it becomes difficult to believe that something you say or do will measure up to become acceptable, important, good enough, or valuable to someone else. For example, when you do not feel worthy, there is a greater tendency for situations that occur in your life to create the belief that you are the following:

- Unloved or unworthy to feel or receive love
- Not good enough or not accepted
- Unattractive
- Unsuccessful or a failure

- Unforgiven or unable to show forgiveness
- Blamed or cursed
- Hopeless or without purpose
- Stupid or insignificant
- Untrusting
- A victim

I'll never forget when I asked a client named Judy to describe what it was like for her to struggle with her sense of worth. Her reply rang true for so many people who come into my office·

> Not being good enough feels like I'm always striving to do better, work harder, and accomplish perfectionism… I'm always comparing myself to others and always wondering if my marriage is going to fail. I need the house to be perfect, which causes chaos within our home. I always make "to-do" lists, and many days I don't get them done, which also makes me feel inadequate and old… There is always something to do or that needs to be done better. Inside, not feeling good enough makes me feel sad, depressed, and many times lonely… My worthless feeling has permeated every facet of my life, even my work, relationships, as well as my purchases. I have to fight constantly to overcome the lack of confidence that I feel.

Like Judy, your worth should not determine how you live your life or how you feel about yourself. Nor should your worth be about who you *should* be in the eyes of others, but rather who you *really* are in the eyes of God. When Jesus died on the cross, your sins were forgiven and you became worthy, deserving, and good enough. Sadly, it was the people and circumstances around you that began the unrealistic expectations or hurtful treatment that created negative thinking and feelings inside. It's time you changed all that. The goal of this book is to declare the truth about who you are. To do this we will declare what God says about you in order for you to live a life full of love, acceptance, success, forgiveness, victory, freedom, trust, significance, confidence, purpose, hope, and much more.

Taking Your Authority

If you want to believe the truth about yourself, now is the time to declare who you really are rather than what you feel you are. The difference with this little book compared to other books that may have been unsuccessful to help you *learn* the truth about yourself is that you will make a decree over yourself. Let me explain. People have been making decrees for centuries. The word *decree* in the original Hebrew language means an edict, statute, or law. It is an official order, a pronouncement, or a legal ruling to effect something. As a child of God, you have royal authority over any evil authority, negative thoughts, beliefs, or feelings that have taken up residence in your life. "Behold, I have given you authority to tread on serpents and scorpions, and over all the power of the enemy, and nothing will injure you" (Luke 10:19).

To take authority over negative areas of your life, you can make a pronouncement to effect a change in how you think and feel. Job 22:28 states, "You will also decree a thing, and it will be established for you; And light will shine on your ways." When you declare what you want, your heavenly Father hears you and wants to give you the desires of your heart. "Trust in the LORD and do good; dwell in the land and cultivate faithfulness. Delight yourself in the LORD; And He will give you the desires of your heart" (Psalm 37:3-4). This book will begin the transformation to renew your mind and heart regarding what you have believed to this point in your life. Whether you believe it or not, God's Word is powerful and your heavenly Father wants the very best for you. It is time you declared your rightful ownership of your worth through your authority in Jesus Christ.

One of the reasons you continue to struggle with the outcome of asking God for your desires (and struggle believing in your self-worth) is that you have not fully accepted or understood the greatness of the authority and power that God has just by declaring something in His name. Unfortunately, many people believe the outcome of their requests is influenced by their own abilities, goodness, or authority. Instead, the outcome of your requests is from the greatness and almighty power of God and what He wants to do for you because He loves you as His child. What affects your prayers and ability to believe goes back to your struggle to believe you are worthy to receive something good. Like most people, the evil authority of negative beliefs and thoughts you have been living under has created a crisis in your ability to believe. One of the purposes of this book is for you to take your rightful authority and cut off the negative influences and evil authority from having any more rights to your thoughts and beliefs.

Praying vs. Declaring

Some of you may be thinking, *Okay, even before I read this book, I've prayed to God in the past and little has changed, so why will this be different?* Although you may have prayed before, chances are you have not *declared* who you are or what you wanted. There is a difference. If you are like most people, when you pray, you are *hoping* for something to happen. So if you *hope* like most people, you are waiting and wishing for something in the future. According to Proverbs 13:12, "Hope deferred makes the heart sick..." So when you hope, you may have a desire, but not the reassurance that something will happen—you hope it will happen.

Please understand I believe prayer is important. However, if you only hope when you pray without the belief or assurance of what God can provide, you can easily become discouraged, which only makes you feel worse. When you *declare* something, according to Job 22:28, you are establishing something, making a proclamation, an announcement, making a decision. In essence, when you are announcing something, you are more apt to believe it, bringing it into a present-tense existence. In addition, you are using your right as a child of the King to take back (declaring) what has been illegally taken from you by the enemy. Jesus not only died on the cross for the salvation of your sins (1 Peter 2:24); He also died for the healing of your diseases and infirmities (Matthew 8:17) and continues to be the path of truth and life (John 14:6). Since God wants to give you the desires of your heart (Proverbs 3:4-6) and nothing is impossible with God (Luke 1:37), what you ask for can become possible when you ask for it (John 15:7). This is why it is time to begin declaring.

When you declare, you must declare with faith, believing that what God says is what He means. That is what Jesus wants you to know when He said, "...All things for which you pray and ask, believe that you have received them, and they will be *granted* you" (Mark 11:24). Unworthiness makes you wonder and doubt if something will happen rather than believe it for now. You are not unworthy anymore because of what God has said about you and what He has done for you on the cross. You are worthy of wellness and wholeness. It's time that you finally believe and proclaim what God wants you to know and believe about yourself When you declare, you are expecting rather than simply hoping, believing what you ask for will happen, even if you don't see it or feel it happening. Isaiah 42:9 states, "Behold, the former things have come to pass, now I declare new things; before they spring forth I proclaim them to you." I believe in you and your ability to declare with the faith of Christ. The fact that you decided to read this book tells me you are *yearning* to grow your faith, and that is enough faith for God to use in order to make a change in your life. Don't wait any longer. God sees your yearning and has been waiting for you to accept what He has for you.

If you allow the words of these declarations to penetrate your heart, you will see His worth, His value, and His love in your life. Together we will *declare* the fact that *who* you are, what you *say*, what you *do*, and what you *think* (everything about you) is worthy, deserving, and good enough.

Opening the Door to Your Declaration

In order to receive what you have full rights to obtain through God, begin reading the following declaration to open the door to greater freedom in Christ. Next, read each of the following declarations to claim who you really are in Christ. Whether you feel or see a change after you first read each declaration is not what is important. It is not what you feel; it is all about what you believe. Simply believe it. That is what faith is all about: simply believing the Word of God for what it says. When you believe God, He will be pleased and want to reward you with more. If you think of a little child you love and adore, don't you want to give them gifts and shower them with good things? That is what your heavenly Father wants to do with you. The more you read over these declarations, the more you will believe them. Begin with this declaration to claim your authority of who you are in Christ:

> I declare I am a child of Almighty God and I am a co-heir of His goodness and mercy through Jesus Christ. All Jesus suffered and paid for on the cross is my inheritance of which I have here on earth. I ask Jesus Christ in my heart as my Lord and Savior to be united with Him. The old has been crucified and buried; the new has risen with Christ and triumphed over the rulers and authorities of evil on earth. Because of His shed blood, I carry the authority over sickness, over sin, over demons, over negative beliefs, and over worldly influences. Because I am one with Christ, I am righteous, I am holy, I am good enough, and I am worthy to receive the truth that God has for me. I choose to accept in my heart, mind, and soul what God wants me to know as I declare His truth for my life.

Declarations

I Am Loved and
I Am Lovable

But God demonstrates His own love toward us, in that while we were yet sinners, Christ died for us.

Romans 5:8

I remember Ellen had tears in her eyes when she told me, "I don't feel loved, and besides, how could someone possibly love me from all the faults that I have?" I was surprised and saddened as I heard that from someone who looked so "put together" from the outside.

To try and understand why she felt that way, I asked, "Why do you think that?"

She said, "I've never told anyone this, but the way I've been treated, I've always thought it was my fault."

I realized that no amount of words would convince Ellen what she had come to believe about herself over the years. She carried inside an unlovable spirit that set up a roadblock from allowing herself to get close enough to be loved by others. Not feeling lovable is often a result of either losing someone's love, not being loved, or ill treatment by the important people in your life. I asked Ellen if she experienced any great loss or hurt in her past. After a minute in thought, she told me with a deep look of sadness on her face how painful it was at eight years old when her parents divorced. She remembered not understanding why her father did not visit her and why her stepfather was so hurtful to her. With tears in her eyes Ellen described how lonely and empty that time was in her life. Often the younger you have a loss or hurt, the more likely you will be affected with issues related to abandonment, rejection, loneliness, and loss. The belief you are unlovable and unworthy to be loved is often the result of these early losses and hurtful experiences.

Ellen cried for some time, as she felt safe enough to finally let go of the hurt she had held inside for so long. I knew the best way to bring healing to the hurt Ellen felt as an adult was to bring healing to the little girl that was still hurting inside. And the best way for the little girl to be healed is for her to be loved. When I asked her to picture Jesus hugging her as an eight-year-old girl, I began to pray for the Holy Spirit to fill Ellen with the Father's love. She began to feel warm inside as she allowed herself, for the first time since eight years old, to experience the warmth of genuine love in her heart.

Similar to Ellen, you may have experienced loss and hurt in your past that caused you to feel unloved or unlovable. Maybe you are experiencing sadness or emptiness you can't seem to fill and just won't go away. God wants you to know how much He loves you and He is saddened that you have felt this way. The good news is God wants you to experience the Father's love by declaring His love for yourself.

Preparing Your Heart to Receive What God Has for You

> My Father in heaven, thank You for what You have done
> on the cross for my life, and I ask Your forgiveness for
> believing that I am unloved. I forgive myself for believ-
> ing I am unloved and not loveable, and I choose to let go
> of the hurt that was caused by this lie. Heavenly Father,
> on the basis of Your forgiveness and Your holy Word, I
> choose to accept that I am loved and receive all that You
> have declared about me. In Jesus's name, I pray.

Declaring the Truth - I Am Loved

As a child of my heavenly Father, I am loved with an everlasting love. I am loved greater than I can ever imagine and greater
than I've ever known. No matter what things I've said or done,
He still loves me. For neither death nor life, neither angels nor
demons, neither my present troubles, nor my future worries,
nor any powers of danger, nor any hardships of life, nor what
anyone has said or done, nor anything else in all creation will be
able to separate me from the love that my heavenly Father has
for me. I am loved so much that He had His Son die for me so
I may live and find abundance of life forever.

My heart is filled to overflowing with all that God has
for me. God is forgiving, good, compassionate, and gracious
toward me whenever I call on Him. I am thankful that God is
slow to anger, abounding in love, and faithful to me. He loves
me so much that He forgives and forgets my sins as far as the
east is from the west.

Because the unfailing love of my heavenly Daddy dwells
within me, I may sing for joy and be glad all my days. I can

think of God standing next to me at all times, helping me in everything I do and say. For His goodness and love will follow me all the days of my life and will dwell with me forever. God's love endures forever, and His faithfulness continues through all my generations. He is a mighty warrior who saves and protects me and takes great delight in me. Because of God's love, I will no longer be judged or rebuked, and I will know that He will rejoice over me with singing and praise. Because of His love, I will abound more and more in knowledge and depth of insight so that I may be able to discern what is best in my life and I may be pure and blameless for each day. I will be filled with the fruit of love, joy, peace, patience, kindness, goodness, faithfulness, gentleness, and self-control that comes through knowing His Son, Jesus Christ. I am encouraged in my heart and united with Christ in love so I may have the full riches of the complete understanding of all the treasures of His wisdom and knowledge in my life. My heavenly Daddy chose me to be His and to be holy and dearly loved by Him, for He will clothe me with compassion, kindness, humility, gentleness, and patience. And over all these virtues, I will put on love to bind them all together in perfect unity. God's mercy, peace, and love will be multiplied in me over and over, forever and ever.

References

Jeremiah 31:3; Romans 8:38-39; John 3:16; Romans 5:8; Ephesians 3:17-19; Psalm 86:5, 15; Revelation 1:5; Psalms 103:12; 90:14; 100:5; 23:6; Zephaniah 3:17; Philippians 1:9; Galatians 5:22-23; Colossians 2:2; 3:12, 14; Jude 1:2

I Am Accepted

Therefore, accept one another, just as Christ also accepted us to the glory of God.

Romans 15:7

Have you ever felt rejected or not accepted? Do you have a gnawing feeling inside that you are not accepted by others whenever you do something? Maybe you didn't get picked for a position you had your heart set on. Maybe you heard (or still hear) words from people in your life who made you feel that you were not wanted. Whatever your experience, I'm here to remind you that you are accepted from the very beginning because God created you, and God does not take kindly to people rejecting His work! Remember, you were worthy, deserving, and good enough because of what Jesus did for you on the cross. It was the people and environment that created any other belief than what God created in you.

Mike had all the appearances of a confident person, but he shared with me his lifelong secret that he struggled with feeling accepted by others, such as friends, coworkers, and even his wife.

"I'm always wondering what people will think about me," Mike emphasized.

When I asked him to describe the feelings in his body at the time he thought about not being accepted, he stared at the floor in silence.

"I guess I feel anxious in my stomach and chest," he finally said with a surprised look on his face.

You see, Mike had felt this way for so long it became part of his life, which made him surprised to find there was a feeling attached to it. I asked him to focus on that feeling as I prayed for the Holy Spirit to take him to an earlier time where he felt it. It didn't take long for childhood memories to come to his mind. Mike remembered never really feeling accepted as a child.

He had memories of his mother making statements such as "You are so stupid" or "Why can't you be more like your brother?" Other sad memories included not being selected for sports teams and little quality time with his father because of his long work hours.

Suddenly, Mike looked up at me and said with a smile of satisfaction, "That's why! I never realized the connection between the lack of time with my parents and my not feeling accepted."

It is very common when the important people in our life are hurtful and/or do not show loving affection and attention, the result can be a lack of acceptance. Mike and I began to work on helping the little boy let go of his sad feelings and ask the Holy Spirit to fill his heart with the heavenly Father's love and acceptance. Just like Mike, God wants you to know and declare how much you are loved and accepted by Him.

Preparing Your Heart to Receive What God Has for You

My Father in heaven, thank You for what You have done on the cross for my life, and I ask Your forgiveness for my lack of belief that You created me to be accepted. I forgive myself for believing I am not accepted, and I choose to let go of the hurt that was caused by others. Heavenly Father, on the basis of Your forgiveness and Your holy Word, I choose to believe that I am accepted and receive all that You have declared about me. In Jesus's name, I pray.

Declaring the Truth - I Am Accepted

My heavenly Father knows my heart and how I have been feeling about myself throughout my life. I am a child of the living God. He loves me and accepts me just the way I am because He created me and does not make mistakes. He loves everyone and does not discriminate between us. God purifies my heart into an accepted heart of faith in Him. He has already approved my works. I am released from any present or past circumstances in which I have been cursed or hurt by any words or experiences that cause my being rejected, unaccepted, unwanted, or abandoned. I forgive anyone in the past and present for causing me to feel unacceptable and release a blessing on them. I am released from the negative emotions and beliefs of these curses and hurts and bind any dark shadow of any evil influence caused by the hurtful experiences. I receive from heaven God's love, acceptance, forgiveness, approval, and blessings upon my life.

My heavenly Father loves me and accepts me, no matter what anyone has said or done to me in the present or past. I am accepted by God because He loves me with an everlasting love, and I have won His approval because I am a child of His. No matter how I am treated in the future, I will be loved, accepted, and blessed by the Holy Spirit as I persevere under trial, and I will receive the crown of life, which the Lord has promised to those who love Him.

I have been approved by God to be entrusted with the gospel so I can speak, not to please people, but to please God. God knows my heart as it is acceptable to Him because He loves me. I do not need to conform to this world, I am transformed by the renewing of my mind as I prove what the will of God is and do the things that are good, acceptable, and perfect before God. God gives me endurance, encouragement, and the same attitude as the mind of Christ. I am able to accept myself and others, just as Christ accepted me, in order to bring praises to God.

References

Acts 15:8-9; Romans 8:16; Ecclesiastes 9:7; Hebrews 11:39; James 1:12; Romans 5:5; 1 Thessalonians 2:4-5; Romans 12:2; Romans 15:5-7

I Can Love Others

Beloved, if God so loved us, we also ought to love one another.

1 John 4:11

Have you or has someone you know struggled with getting emotionally close or showing affection, such as hugs and kisses? What many people don't know is that showing affection to others should be something that comes as easy as taking your next breath. However, if your primary caregivers did not show you love or role model how to give affection, loving others will not come very easy. In fact, if your caregivers did not receive love from the generation before them, chances are there is a generational pattern of broken heartedness that has made its way to you that needs to be cut off. Even the Bible tells that the sins and problems of our caregivers will be passed on to the next generation (Jeremiah 32:18 and Deuteronomy 5:9).

I remember Roger walked slowly as he came limping into my office with a very sad and tired look on his face. When I inquired about why he was limping, he said he'd had a pain in his hip for years and the doctors had not been able to find the cause. Roger was resigned to live with hip pain for the rest of his life.

When I asked him what he wanted to talk about, he said, "My marriage is on the verge of divorce, and I don't know what to do." When I asked what he thought were some of the reasons for his situation, he immediately told me, "I've struggled for years with showing love and affection to my wife, and I realized I didn't listen when she wanted me to change."

After years of feeling frustrated, unloved, and empty, his wife finally told him she was done with the marriage. The shock of his wife giving up devastated Roger, which broke him to the point of finally realizing what he was *not* doing in the relationship.

It is often the case that when we are at a crisis point in our lives, we are ready to make deeper changes to former stubborn behaviors. And that is the time we are willing to allow God to help us. When I asked the Holy Spirit to take Roger back to where he first felt this type of loss, interestingly, Roger saw an image of himself as a little boy with his mother standing off to the distance. At that very moment, Roger realized his struggle to show love originated from his mother not showing love to him. His eyes began showing tears as he said, "My mother was always busy and seemed never there for me." Roger suddenly realized the emptiness he felt throughout his adult life was the same feeling he had as a little boy. When I asked Roger to envision Jesus with the little boy, he began feeling a warmth radiate throughout his body as he envisioned Jesus putting His arms around the little boy. During this experience, I prayed for the Holy Spirit to pour the Father's love in a greater way over Roger as he thought about himself as a little boy.

At that moment, the Holy Spirit brought to my attention the need to pray for the pain in Roger's hip.

I said to Roger, "The Holy Spirit loves you so much He wants you to be healed emotionally and physically." I continued in prayer. "Because You love him, Holy Spirit, I ask that You bring total healing in his life. Heal his heart, bring healing to his hip, and send away the pain. In Jesus's name."

After Roger wiped his tearstained face, he said with a big smile that he felt a warm feeling in his heart and the pain in his hip was gone! Praise God for what He can do! Roger had a love encounter for the first time within his heart that changed him emotionally, physically, and spiritually. When he received the love from the heavenly Father, for the first time, Roger's heart could feel love. As a result, he was able to give love in a way he was not able in the past. Just like with Roger, God loves you and wants you to receive His love so you can give that love away to others.

Preparing Your Heart to Receive What God Has for You

In the name of Jesus, I bind any generational curses of brokenheartedness and remove any hindrances from receiving love in my heart. Holy Spirit, open my heart to receive what God has declared about me, and fill my heart with the love of my heavenly Father. In Jesus's name, I pray.

Declaring the Truth - I Can Love Others

Heavenly Father has given me a new heart and a new spirit within me. He removed my heart of stone and gives me a new heart of flesh. Because of the new heart, I will walk in the way of love, as God has given me His love through His Son, Jesus Christ. My love will abound more and more in knowledge and depth so I will discern how to love others. I will not be discouraged, doubt, fear, or be intimidated about loving others because the Holy Spirit will be with me. I will not allow the sins of my past and the generations before me to block my ability to love others. I turn away from all my offenses; then sin will not be my downfall. In Christ, I am rid of all the offenses I have committed, and I receive a new heart and a new spirit from my heavenly Father. I choose to love because God first loved me and showed His love to me through His one and only Son. I choose to love through the example of Jesus. My mouth will speak words of wisdom, and the meditation of my heart will give me understanding. I will rejoice in everything I do and be reassured in how I feel. I choose to be likeminded with Christ in how I think, and I will live in a sweet peace as I allow the God of love and peace to be with me as I show His love to others.

I will walk in a manner worthy with which God has called me; I will walk with all humility, and gentleness, and patience, showing tolerance for one another in love. The Holy Spirit helps guard my heart, mind, and spirit as I remain in the peace of God. I choose to love and live in peace with others knowing I am one spirit in Christ. I have great expectations of loving in ways God wants me to love. The Lord will make my love increase and overflow for others as I hold others in the highest regard in love because of who they are in Christ. Because God is just, He will remember my work and the love I will show as I continue to help and love His people. The grace of the Lord Jesus Christ and the love of God and the fellowship of the Holy Spirit will be with me in whatever I do and say.

References

Ezekiel 36:26; Ephesians 5:2; Philippians 1:9-11; 1 John 4:9-16, 19; Ezekiel 18:30-31; 2 Corinthians 13:11; Psalm 49:3; Ephesians 4:1-4; 1 Thessalonians 3:12; 5:13; Hebrews 6:10; 2 Corinthians 13:14

I Am Worthy

...Walk in a manner worthy of the Lord, to please Him in all respects, bearing fruit in every good work and increasing in the knowledge of God.

Colossians 1:10

What do you think or say when someone gives you a compliment? Do you shrug off kind words as if they are untrue? Does a compliment make you feel uncomfortable and embarrassed or make you feel happy and good about yourself? Did you know that how you respond to a compliment is usually how you feel about yourself? Your response should be one of acceptance, pleasure, and appreciation. Unfortunately, many people do not feel or believe they are worthy or good enough to receive a compliment. When you do not feel worthy about yourself, you struggle to receive good things from others. My question is, where did all this start in you?

What you received from the important people in your life has everything to do with how worthy and important you may feel the rest of your life. Think about it: when someone you believe is important shows you attention and treats you importantly, then you will come to believe there must be something worthwhile, valuable, and important about yourself. How others treat you is the beginning of what you believe about yourself.

One Sunday I attended my church after speaking at a faith seminar. During the service I gave a testimony of how God miraculously restored the hearing to a woman that I prayed for at the seminar. When the service was over, a woman named Janice came to me and said that during my testimony, God told her that her own hearing would be restored. She had been affected with a hearing loss for many years and had to wear hearing aids. Janice asked if I would pray to restore her hearing. After I commanded her ears to open and her hearing to be restored, I then asked if she noticed anything different. With her eyes filling with tears, Janice leaned closer as if telling me a secret. She quietly said, "I don't feel worthy for God to heal me." It broke my heart that she could not accept what God so freely wanted to give her. What was interesting was that even though she believed enough to sense God leading her to ask me for healing, her personal feelings of not being worthy overpowered God's revelation. It is often the case that ungodly thoughts or hurt emotion that we carry inside will overpower our ability to believe godly truth. When the negative thoughts and emotion are identified and eliminated, God's truth can become more real in your heart. And as a result, you will live out what you believe.

After I shared how much God loved her and cut off the spirit of unworthiness, we prayed again for her healing. Immediately, Janice began hearing a difference in both her ears. Similar to Janice, God loves you too much to have you settle with less than

His truth about you. He wants you to know of your worthiness and wants you to have and declare what is yours to receive.

Preparing Your Heart to Receive What God Has for You

> My Father in heaven, thank You for what You have done on the cross for my life, and I ask Your forgiveness for my lack of belief in what You created in me. I forgive myself for believing the lie of unworthiness, and I choose to let go of the hurt that was caused by this lie. Heavenly Father, on the basis of Your forgiveness and holy Word, I choose to accept that I am worthy and receive all that You have declared about me. In Jesus's name, I pray.

Declaring the Truth - I Am Worthy

I am filled with the knowledge of God's will, with all spiritual wisdom and understanding, so that I will walk in a manner worthy of the Lord, to please Him in all respects. I am worthy to bear fruit in every good work that I do. I am strengthened with all power according to His glorious might, for the attaining of all steadfastness and patience, joyously giving thanks to the Father, who has qualified me to share in the inheritance of what God has for me. I walk in a manner worthy of the calling with which I have been called by the gospel of Christ. I stand firm with all humility, gentleness, and patience, showing tolerance for one another in love, being careful to protect the unity of the Spirit in the bond of peace with others.

In Christ, I have the authority to bind, break off, and cast away from my life every word curse, orphan spirit, and hurtful action that has been brought against me by people in my past or present. In Christ, I am able to bind and remove anything that is blocking my heart and mind from receiving all the worthiness, goodness, and forgiveness that God has for me. I choose to forgive the people who caused every word curse, hurt, and disappointment and ask for forgiveness for what I have caused against another person. I receive the blessings of my heavenly Father's inheritance of love, worthiness, goodness, and faithfulness for the healing of my heart, mind, and soul.

I am considered worthy of the kingdom of God and walk in a manner worthy of the God Who calls me into His own kingdom and glory. I am precious in the sight of God. He honors me and loves everything about me because I am created in His image. I have nothing to fear, for God is with me and I am loved by God with an everlasting love. I am worthy because I am more valuable than the sparrows and the Lord knows the number of the very hairs on my head. I accept the Word of God for what it really is and it will perform its work in me. God fulfills every desire for goodness in my life. God counts me worthy for the work of faith with power so that the name of our Lord Jesus will be glorified in me according to the grace of our God and the Lord Jesus Christ.

References

Colossians 1:9-13; Ephesians 4:1-3; Philippians 1:26; 2 Thessalonians 1:5, 11-12; Isaiah 43:4-5; Genesis 1:27; Jeremiah 31:3; Matthew 10:30-31; 2 Thessalonians 1:11-12

I Have an
Inheritance of Blessings

We have obtained an inheritance, having been predestined according to His purpose who works all things after the counsel of His will.

Ephesians 1:11

How many times have you heard comments from people such as "You act just like your father" or "You're so stupid"? And how many times have you made a negative comment to yourself, such as "That was so dumb" or "I'm going to fail"?

Have you grown up in a family that has a generational pattern of abuse, lack of love and affection, overly strict discipline, strict religious beliefs, emotional outbursts, divorce, an absent parent, or other negative experiences? These experiences act like a curse, attaching themselves to your heart, mind, and/or spirit, which can become a self-fulfilling prophecy in ways you do not see. The more you have negative experiences with the important people in your life, the more likely you will inherit the beliefs and feelings associated with those experiences. In short, your spirit and self-worth is crushed when you are physically or emotionally hurt by someone important in your life. Unless they are cut off, curses are often inherited from one generation to the next with little detection of how devastating they can be.

I remember talking to a client in my office named Joe. He said, with a puzzled look on his face, "I have a hard time finishing a project because I never feel like what I do is good enough." When I asked Joe if he ever made negative comments about himself, he said, a little embarrassed, "I often say things like, 'That was stupid' or 'This is never going to work.'"

I asked him where that type of negative thinking might have come from.

Joe stood there looking puzzled for a moment before he blurted out loud, "Now I remember. That was what my dad said to me all the time. You know, I hated it when he said that!"

After all these years, Joe continued to berate himself just as his father did.

I said to Joe, "That means you're acting just like your father."

Joe didn't like that statement. Especially since he said he didn't want to be in any way like his father. I told Joe that his father's hurtful words were the original curse over him. Unfortunately, the curse continued through Joe's actions and words about his abilities that were similar to his father's. The negative messages received as a child became the same messages he used toward himself as an adult.

Joe said he was ready to finally free himself of the word curses from his past. He repeated a prayer to cut off the generational curses of negative words and actions from his parents. Over time Joe began to recognize a change in the way he looked at life. He had a better appreciation for his own work and became less critical of himself and others.

If you feel or believe there are any negative words or actions that you do to yourself or others, God wants you to be free from what you have inherited. Ephesians 1:3-4 states that we have obtained an inheritance from our Lord Jesus Christ, who has blessed us with every spiritual blessing in the heavenly places in Him, just as He chose us in Him before the foundation of the world that we would be holy and blameless before Him in love. Now that's an inheritance! You can declare your rightful inheritance from your heavenly Father right now.

Preparing Your Heart to Receive What God Has for You

My Father in heaven, thank You for what You have done on the cross for my life, and I ask Your forgiveness for not believing in Your inheritance for my life. I forgive myself and others for not believing in my inheritance. Heavenly Father, on the basis of Your forgiveness and Your holy Word, I choose to accept my inheritance from heaven and receive all that You have declared about me. In Jesus's name, I pray.

Declaring the Truth - I Have an Inheritance

I am blessed by the heavenly Father with every spiritual blessing in the heavenly places in Jesus Christ. God decided in advance to adopt me as a child into His heavenly family through His Son, Jesus Christ. God did this out of His great kindness and love for me. I am holy and blameless before Him in love. I am a child of the king, heir of God, and co-heir with Jesus to the greatness, power, and glory that is available through my reward of the inheritance in the heavenly realms. I am glad and leap for joy, for my reward is great in heaven.

The blood of Jesus stands as a wall of separation between me and every curse, ungodly statement, and ungodly covenant made by the generations before me I remove every right of the demonic to afflict me because of those sins. I call to me my righteous inheritance and the heavenly blessings my Father has for me.

The eyes of my heart are enlightened to know what the hope of God's calling is and to know all the riches of the glory of His inheritance that are available to me. And to be filled with the knowledge of God's will in all spiritual wisdom and understanding so that I will walk in a manner worthy of the Lord to please Him in all respects, bearing fruit in every good work and increasing in the knowledge of God. I will be strengthened with all power, according to His glorious might, for the attaining of all steadfastness and patience, joyously giving thanks to the Father, who has qualified me to share in His inheritance in the heavenly realms. For God rescued me from the domain of darkness and brought me to the kingdom of His beloved Son, in whom I have deliverance and the forgiveness of sins. Whatever I do for the Lord, I know I will receive His reward of His inheritance because it is the Lord Christ whom I serve. I am strong and will not lose courage in what I do for the Lord, for I will receive a reward for my work as presented unto the Lord. My inheritance will never perish, spoil, or fade and is shielded by God's power until the coming of the salvation that is ready to be revealed in the last days.

References

Ephesians 1:3-5; Romans 8:17; Luke 6:23; Colossians 3:24; Ephesians 1:18, Colossians 1:9-14; 3:24; 2 Chronicles 15:7; 1 Peter 3-4

I Am Blameless

Just as He chose us in Him before the foundation of the world, that we would be holy and blameless before Him In love

Ephesians 1:4

Do you know anyone who apologizes for everything, even if there is little need for an apology? Maybe you always feel like you have done something wrong or wonder if you have. This is very common for people who have grown up or currently live (or work) in an environment where negative comments, blaming, and fault-finding are regular occurrences. These atmospheres often create shame-based thinking, where you are always second-guessing yourself, believing you are to blame or did something wrong if there is the slightest question about anything. In fact, you may still be blaming yourself for something that happened years ago. If you did not have forgiving people in your life, whether in the past or present, you will continue the tradition on yourself. The good news is, when you decide to sincerely forgive yourself, those who hurt you, and forgive God, you become forgiven and blameless. It's that simple. In fact, Jesus died for your sins so you don't have to carry that around anymore. If you keep blaming yourself, you become no different than the people who originally blamed and hurt you. It is time you begin forgiving yourself and allow what Jesus did on the cross to be the releasing power for your forgiveness.

When Doug came to see me, he shared his guilt and sadness about the auto accident he was involved in several years ago in which another person was hurt. Even though what happened was an accident and Doug was not at fault, he continued to have constant remorse and questions about whether he could have done something different that may have spared the other person from becoming hurt. Even as Doug tried to work through what happened, he continued to question himself and his decisions about everything. As we talked it seemed no amount of words could convince Doug of what he had come to believe—that he was to blame and should have changed the outcome. Similar to Doug, I have found that it is very common for people to struggle with a negative belief as long as they hold on to the negative emotions that surround that event.

Doug had mixed emotions of sadness and anger as he described details of the accident. "I will never forget what happened," he said as he shook his head in disbelief.

When I asked Doug to picture what Jesus would say or do as He sat next to him in the car, suddenly, a great sobbing of tears began to flow as he held his face with his hands.

"He's telling me it's okay now. I don't have to hold on to it any longer," Doug said with a big sigh of relief. "Jesus said it wasn't my fault."

I asked the Holy Spirit to bring understanding as to why Doug had difficulty letting go of blaming himself. Doug didn't hesitate to think of his mother's voice as she frequently blamed him for his little brother getting hurt. He learned how strongly his thinking and believing were influenced by the experiences in his past.

At that moment Doug realized he could forgive himself. Jesus had freed him from his inner turmoil of blame, shame, and remorse.

If you are feeling guilt, remorse, blame, or burdened, you do not deserve to feel that way. You can make the choice to forgive yourself. When you accept what Jesus did in your heart and ask Him to help release the pain, you will be better able to ask for help to let go.

Preparing Your Heart to Receive What God Has for You

My Father in heaven, thank You for what You have done on the cross for my life, and I ask Your forgiveness for my lack of belief that You died so I may be blameless. I forgive myself for believing I am to be judged and blamed, and I forgive others for the way they treated me. Heavenly Father, on the basis of Your forgiveness and Your holy Word, I choose to accept that I am blameless and receive all that You have declared about me. In Jesus's name, I pray.

Declaring the Truth - I Am Blameless

I am blameless in my ways from the day I was created and am blameless before the Lord my God because of what Jesus did for me on the cross. I receive the grace that He gives to me in Christ Jesus. Everything I have is enriched in every way—I have the ability to speak about my faith and have all the knowledge into the meaning of faith. I am not lacking in any spiritual gift as I eagerly await the revelation of my Lord Jesus Christ. I am strong to the end so that I will be blameless on the day when Jesus Christ returns. God is faithful and has called me into fellowship with his Son, Jesus Christ our Lord.

God has blessed me with every spiritual blessing in the heavenly places in Christ. Before the creation of the world, God chose me to be with Him to be holy and blameless in His sight. God decided in advance to adopt me into His heavenly family through what Jesus Christ did for me on the cross because this is what God wanted to do for me. In Him, I have redemption through His blood, the forgiveness of sins, in accordance with the riches of God's grace. I can do everything without grumbling or arguing because I am blameless and pure. I choose to let go and forgive myself of any self-blame and let go and forgive any blame I have on others. I choose to forgive anyone who has blamed me and I ask forgiveness from God for any blame that I have carried.

God sees me without blame or blemish. With the grace of God, I can do what is righteous, I can speak the truth from my heart, my tongue utters no slander, and I can do no wrong to a neighbor and cast no slur on others. Regardless what I have done in the past, there is no condemnation, for I am in Christ Jesus. For the law of the spirit of life in Christ Jesus has set me free from the law of sin and of death. I have been made right through my faith in God; I have peace with Him through my Lord Jesus Christ. I have gained access by faith into the grace in which I have with Him. I praise God in my hope of experiencing and enjoying the glory of Him of which I receive as my inheritance from God in heaven. For the Lord God is my sun and shield. The Lord bestows favor and honor and gives me forgiveness and all good things from my walk is blameless. I can trust in the Lord Almighty.

References

Ezekiel 28:15; Deuteronomy 18:13; 1 Corinthians 1-9; Ephesians 1:3-7, Philippians 2:14-16; Psalm 15:3-5; Ephesians 2:13; Romans 5:1-2; Romans 8:1-2; Psalm 84:11-12

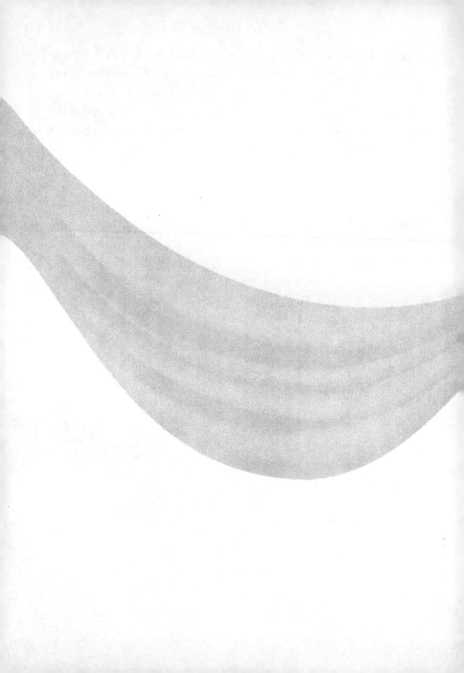

I Am Wonderfully Made

For we are His workmanship, created in Christ Jesus for good works, which God prepared beforehand so that we would walk in them.

Ephesians 2:10

Whatever you may feel or believe about yourself, I want you to know something very important. I want to tell you that I know without a shadow of a doubt that you are good enough as a person and deserving of good things in your life. Do you know why I believe this so strongly? Because God is the one Who created you good enough. As the saying goes, God doesn't make junk, and you were not created as a mistake.

Have you ever had one of those experiences where you begin questioning or doubting yourself? I had an experience as early as fifth grade that altered my belief about myself for many years. Sitting at my desk one particular day, I could see the anger rise in our teacher's face after the kids in the class did not respond like she wanted. In a gruff intimidating voice, the teacher burst out the words, "You kids will never amount to anything when you grow up!"

I could feel my heart race as I became afraid. As a ten-year-old, my heart sank into despair. *Maybe I won't amount to anything*, I thought as her words rang over and over in my ears. *She must be right; after all, she is my teacher.*

I know I tried to get over that terrible day by stuffing her words away with all the other experiences in my past. But what was different about this memory was her words seemed to have a power and authority that questioned my very being. I never realized how much those words negatively affected how I believed in myself. I found her words haunting me for years after I left that class, like a dark cloud of doubt that hung over me. I reacted to life from what I believed—questioning myself, like a constant nagging doubt. It was not until I began working through that memory as an adult and learned my true value through a relationship with Jesus Christ that I realized this: no matter what anyone says, I know I am wonderfully made in God's image and I do not need to rely on someone else's opinion.

What about you? If you struggle with what to believe about yourself, you need to rely on how God created you and what He said about you rather than relying on what others have said or done. God wants you to know the truth: you are a wonderful, deserving, and good enough person—He created you that way.

Preparing Your Heart to Receive What God Has for You

My Father in heaven, thank You for what You have done on the cross for my sake, and I ask Your forgiveness for my lack of belief in You and the wonderful way You made me. I forgive myself for believing the past lies, and I forgive those who contributed to those lies.

Heavenly Father, on the basis of Your forgiveness and Your holy Word, I choose to accept that I am wonderfully made and receive all that You have declared about me. In Jesus's name, I pray.

Declaring the Truth - I Am Wonderfully Made

The heavenly Father knows me better than anyone. He knows when I sit and when I rise up. He perceives my thoughts from wherever I am. He can discern whatever I do and is familiar with all my ways before I even do them. God knows me so well that before a word is on my tongue, He knows it completely. I give thanks, for I am wonderfully made in the image of God. I am wonderfully made because of His works in heaven, and my inner soul knows it very well. My frame was not hidden from Him when I was made. His eyes saw my unformed body before anyone else, and greatness of all the future days that were ordained for my life were written in His book before I came to be. How precious to me are His ways and His thoughts! God has so many good thoughts about me that if I were to count them, they would outnumber the grains of sand on the earth.

God created me in His own image. He made me in His likeness, and He wants to bless me. Because God is rich in mercy over me and has a great love for me, when I was dead in my sins, He made me alive in order that I may be together with Christ and seat me with Him in the heavenly places. I am God's handiwork, created in Christ Jesus to do good works that God prepared in advance for me to do. For God created my inmost being and knitted me together in my mother's womb. Because Jesus Christ died for me, I am able to put away the old negative thinking and put on the new positive beliefs about who I am. I am assured that I am created to have true righteousness and holiness that God wants for me.

In Christ all things were created—things in heaven and on earth, visible and invisible, whether thrones or powers or rulers or authorities, and that means even I have been created through Christ and for Christ. For everything—yes, everything—God created is good, and that includes me. Nothing is to be rejected if it is received with thanksgiving. God is worthy to receive glory and honor and power, for I was created by God, and I am so glad that He included me. The ravens do not have to plant or gather food and have no storeroom to put the food, yet God feeds them all they need. If God can provide for the little ravens with such love and care, God will take care of my needs since He considers me much more valuable than the birds! I will give thanks to God, for I am fearfully and wonderfully made; wonderful are His works, and my soul knows it very well. I thank God for wonderfully making me and caring for all my needs.

References

Psalm 139:13; Luke 12:24; Genesis 1:27; 5:1; Ephesians 2:4; 2:10; 4:24; Colossians 1:16; 1 Timothy 4:4; Revelation 4; 11; Genesis 9:6; 2 Corinthians 9:8; Psalm 139:14

I Am Forgiven

Let it be known to you, brethren, that through Him forgiveness of sins is proclaimed to you...

Acts 13:38

When you do not feel worthy, you often do not believe you
are deserving of forgiveness. You may feel you are a second-
class citizen, not allowed to have the same rights that everyone
else is allowed to have. So when circumstances happen that are
an accident or out of your control, even if you did everything
to the best of your ability, you still question your actions and
would not be able to forgive yourself.

Susan shared about feeling a little ache of sadness deep
inside that she couldn't get rid of. She usually can live life without thinking of it but expressed her being tired of struggling
with this feeling that has taunted her for years. When we asked
the Holy Spirit to reveal any events that may have been the origin of this emotion, the thought came to her about an abortion
she had many, many years ago.

"But I let that go a long time ago," was her answer and the
frequent belief I hear for this issue. When I asked Susan if she

ever forgave herself, she became silent as she looked to the floor trying hold back the tears.

As she wiped her eyes, she said, "How could I forgive myself when I don't even believe God would?"

Susan put the feelings away so long ago she never resolved the fact she could not forgive herself because of the terrible, unforgivable act she believed she committed.

When there is unforgiveness, it is common to be consumed with guilt, unresolved emotion, and with a fear of what others think and what God thinks of us. These beliefs and emotions can hinder you from moving toward forgiveness and moving on with life. When Susan was able to cry out the unresolved emotion and ask God for help to forgive herself, she was able to begin truly letting go. God wants you to be free to experience forgiveness. Do not let what you believe you have done or what has happened get in the way of what God can do to free you from that bondage. You deserve to be forgiven because Jesus died on the cross for your forgiveness. If you do not accept forgiveness, the suffering and death of Jesus on the cross was for nothing.

Preparing Your Heart to Receive What God Has for You

My Father in heaven, thank You for what You have done on the cross for my life, and I ask Your forgiveness for holding on to unforgiveness. In Jesus's name, I choose to let go of any hurt that has hindered me from forgiving myself and others. Heavenly Father, on the basis of Your forgiveness and Your holy Word, I receive all that You have declared about me. In Jesus's name, I pray.

Declaring the Truth - I Am Forgiven

I am forgiven because I choose at this moment to ask for forgiveness of my sins of the past and present through my Lord and Savior, Jesus Christ. Just as the man who was hanging on a cross next to Jesus was immediately forgiven for his sins when he asked, I am forgiven because I ask. God loves me so much that I can rest in the reassurance that after God forgives me, He will not remember what I have done as far as the east is from the west. God is gracious, compassionate, slow to anger, and abounding in loving-kindness. Because I believe in Christ, I receive forgiveness of my sins and redemption of my soul. Through Him, I am freed from all things from which I could not be freed from the things of the world. I choose to let all bitterness, wrath, anger, clamor, slander, and malice be let go from me. I choose to forgive those in my past who hurt me, disappointed me, and were not there for me. I choose to open my heart and mind again to love and trust other people. I choose be kind to others, tender-hearted, forgiving others, just as God in Christ also has forgiven me. Just as I forgive others, God will also forgive me.

Because God has forgiven me, I choose to forgive myself of anything I have done wrong to anyone knowingly or unknowingly in the past and present. I have the choice to let go and learn what to do better the next time. I do not need to endure what I feel inside because of a mistake I have made or what someone else did or said to me. I am allowed to make mistakes and forgive myself for what I have done. I choose to give myself permission to heal and love myself. I can forgive others who have hurt me because God has forgiven me and He wants the best for me. I choose freedom and grace in my life because I choose to forgive instead of living in judgment and torment from any unforgiveness that may be in my life. I choose life with forgiveness rather than death with unforgiveness. I am worthy to be forgiven by God and to receive all forgiveness and blessings that God has for my life.

References

Psalm 32:1; Nehemiah 9:17; Acts 10:43; 13:37-39; Ephesians 4:31-32; Mark 11:25

I Am Victorious

> For whatever is born of God overcomes the world; and
> this is the victory that has overcome the world—our faith.
>
> 1 John 5:4

When you don't feel worthy, you may feel you just cannot seem
to win. The harder you try to make something work, the more
something negative seems to happen. Or you constantly feel like
you're a victim on the losing side of life. You may become frustrated and feel so defeated you just want to give up. Maybe you
are going through many difficulties—like you are fighting a battle and you feel discouraged about life. If you have felt anything
like this at any time in your life, you are certainly not alone.

For the past ten years, Betty had severe chronic pain from
osteoporosis throughout her body, especially her legs. The arthritis and deformity in her feet were so severe she could not walk
without pain, and her toes were turned to a forty-five degree
angle. Since I am aware that eighty to ninety percent of medical
ailments have a psychological root, I asked Betty what happened
ten years ago (which is when her conditions apparently began).

She said that is when her husband died. Betty continued to share about the multiple physical and emotional abuses over her lifetime, especially from the people who were closest to her. As a result, Betty felt like a victim suffering with pain and medical conditions for most of her life. She was tired of feeling miserable from these afflictions and was desperate for God to bring healing and restoration in her heart and body. After Betty released her emotional pain from years of abuse, she was able to begin the process of forgiving those who hurt her. When she was free from the emotional bitterness and unforgiveness, I asked if she wanted me to pray for physical healing. With tears in her eyes, she gave a resounding, "Yes." When I commanded the osteoporosis and arthritis to leave in Jesus's name, the pain in her body completely left. For the first time in years, she was able to walk with no pain! Betty spoke to me by phone later in the week to report that the morning after our session, she woke up and her toes were fifty percent straighter. When Betty decided to let go and let God take over, she went from victim to victory. Praise God!

Whatever your circumstance, and whatever you feel physically or emotionally, God loves you and wants you to become victoriously free. Jesus died on the cross to take away your sins, hurts, and diseases. When you accept Jesus in your heart and ask Him to help you release the pain and declare a change in your circumstances, you can become more than an overcomer— you can become victorious.

Preparing Your Heart to Receive What God Has for You

My Father in heaven, thank You for what You have done on the cross for my life, and I ask Your forgiveness for not believing in what You did to give me victory over my circumstances. I forgive myself for not believing in my victory. Heavenly Father, on the basis of Your forgiveness and Your holy Word, I choose to accept that I am victorious and receive all that You have declared about me. In Jesus's name, I pray.

Declaring the Truth - I Am Victorious

My Heavenly Father gives me the desire of my heart and makes all my plans succeed.

I sing for joy over my victory and lift up my banners in the name of our God. The Lord grants all my requests. Now this I know: The Lord gives victory to His anointed. He answers me from His heavenly sanctuary with the victorious power of His right hand. I let go of anything hindering me from receiving my victory in Jesus Christ. I believe in the victory that Christ has for me. I forgive those who have hurt me and try to come against me. The Lord is my rock, my fortress, and my deliverer; my God is my rock, in whom I take refuge, my shield, and the horn of my salvation, my stronghold. God is my refuge, my strength, and my help in trouble. The Lord my God is in my midst. As a victorious warrior, He exults over me with joy. He is quiet in His love, and He rejoices over me with shouts of joy.

When I go into battle against my enemies, I will not be fainthearted or afraid. I will not panic or be terrified by my enemies. I will not fear, for the Lord is with me. I am strong in the Lord with His mighty power. I put on the full armor of God and take a stand against the devil's schemes. For my struggle is not against flesh and blood but against the rulers, against the authorities, against the powers of this dark world, and against the spiritual forces of evil in the heavenly realms. I put on the full armor of God so that when the day of evil comes, I am able to stand my ground. I stand firm with the belt of truth buckled around my waist, with the breastplate of righteousness in place, and with my feet fitted with the readiness that comes from the gospel of peace. In addition to all this, I take up the shield of faith, with which I extinguish all the flaming arrows of the evil one before they come against me. I take the helmet of salvation and the sword of the Spirit, which is the Word of God to speak truth with those around me. I will pray in the Spirit on all occasions with all kinds of prayers and requests glorifying His name.

I will not need to be anxious, for the Lord is my God who will strengthen me and help me. The Lord is the one who goes with me to fight against my enemies to give me victory. I have the reassurance that in Christ I have the victory that has overcome the world. I will go forth victoriously in the cause of truth, humility, and justice. I will go forth and achieve awesome deeds. My heavenly Father gives me victory over my enemies and will put my adversaries to shame. In God, I can boast all day long and will praise His name forever. God gives me aid against the enemy, for human help is worthless. But with God I will gain the victory, and He will trample down my enemies.

References

Psalm 20:4-6; Isaiah 41:10; Psalm 18:2; Zephaniah 3:17; Deuteronomy 20:3-4; Ephesians 6:10-18; Isaiah 41:10; 1 John 5:4; Psalm 45:3-4; 46:1; Psalm 44:5-8; 60:11-12

I Am Free

For the law of the Spirit of life in Christ Jesus has set you free from the law of sin and of death.

Romans 8:2

When I think of the opposite of *freedom*, I come up with *bondage*. Like so many people, you may be held in captivity by something or someone and don't even know it. You may be involved in a relationship or habit-forming activity that controls your time, energy, health, money, or focus in life. These represent a form of bondage to something you may or may not see. Whether you are trapped in unhealthy habits, relationships, or emotional and physical conditions, God wants you to know that in spite of your situation, He loves you and wants to help you live a free and healthy life.

Maryann told me she felt sad and a heaviness inside with little motivation or desire to do much of anything. When I asked how long she felt this way, she had a sad look on her face as she said, "I guess most of my life."

When we asked the Holy Spirit to bring more understanding, an image of sitting in a jail cell came to Maryann. I asked if there was ever a time when she had a feeling as if being confined in a jail cell, the image of cleaning the house and caring for her siblings as a little girl came to mind. When I asked Jesus to come and show the little girl what she needed to know, Maryann began to cry. Jesus said she didn't have to hold on to the burden of feeling responsible for everything anymore. When we asked Jesus for more revelation, Maryann saw a key in the jail cell door.

When I asked Maryann why she had been sitting in the cell all these years, she said, "I didn't know I could leave by letting it go."

Maryann had been living in the bondage of inappropriate responsibility for so long she never realized she could be free. When she prayed for an emotional release and declared her freedom, she pictured the jail cell door wide open and her walking out with Jesus into freedom.

You too have the opportunity of finding freedom. God wants you to use the freedom of choice He gave you to exercise your ability to have healthy changes in your life by seeking healthy solutions and standing on the declaration of your freedom to be healthy. If you feel stuck, depressed, in bondage, or unmotivated, you can become free. Ask the Holy Spirit where you felt this way before and begin to release those earlier feelings to Jesus.

Preparing Your Heart to Receive What God Has for You

My Father in heaven, thank You for what You have done on the cross to free me from any bondage in my life. I ask for Your forgiveness for my lack of belief in Your Word, which states I am free. I forgive myself for not believing in my freedom. Heavenly Father, on the basis of Your forgiveness and Your holy Word, I choose to accept that I am free from anything that has held me in bondage and receive all that You have declared about me. In Jesus's name, I pray.

Declaring the Truth - I Am Free

I have freedom because Jesus Christ set me free when He died on the cross for my sins. I can stand firm and not allow myself to become burdened again by the yoke from heavy chains of my past. In Jesus Christ I am released of negative habit-forming activities that control my time, energy, health, money, or focus in life. In Christ, I am released from the bondage of emotional conditions that negatively consume my life. In Christ, I am released from the hurtful words and actions of the people in my life and the generations before me that created the lies of believing I was trapped or in bondage to anyone or anything. I forgive myself for thinking and believing these lies. I choose to forgive and release all those who have contributed to forming these lies in my life and ask the Father in heaven to send a blessing to them in its place. I receive from heaven the love of God, my Father. I receive my heavenly inheritance of freedom from bondage because of what Christ did on the cross for me. And I receive all the blessings and freedom that come with being associated with the King.

God loves me and opens the door to my freedom through Jesus Christ, for Jesus is the way, the truth, and the life for my salvation and eternal life of freedom. I am a new creation in Christ. The old has gone; the new is here! There is now no condemnation for me in Christ Jesus. I am a new person freed from my sinful actions, thoughts, and words of my past. I am freed from the sinful acts, thoughts, and words of others, for the law of the spirit of life in Christ Jesus has set me free from the law of sin and of death. I do not need to live according to the negative thinking, trapped feelings, or sinful acts. Rather, I choose to live according to the Spirit and set my mind on whatever is true, whatever is honorable, whatever is right, whatever is pure, whatever is lovely, whatever is of good repute, and anything worthy of praise. My mind will dwell on these things, and I will practice these things of Christ and the God of peace will be with me. I am set free to move forward in my life with Christ. I have the reassurance of my freedom because my heavenly Father loves me and has released me from my sins by His shed blood on the cross and has made me to be a priest to serve his God and Father—to Him be the glory and power forever and ever!

References

Galatians 5:1; 1 Peter 2:24; John 14:6; Romans 8:1-5; 2 Corinthians 5:16; Philippians 4:8-9; Revelation 1:5-6

I Am Significant

Therefore you are no longer a slave, but a son; and if a
son, then an heir through God.

Galatians 4:7

Thinking back in your life, did you ever feel like no one wanted
to play with you or someone else was favored more than you,
or your efforts seemed to be overlooked by others? Hurtful
situations like these often create the feeling you are invisible,
unwanted, nobody, don't belong, or not important. In fact,
when you feel this way long enough, it becomes a way of life! I
want to make sure you know you are somebody important, no
matter what you have come to feel or believe. Because of what
God has done through His Son, Jesus Christ, you can declare
you are significant.

I remember when Amy told me she felt a lack of connection
with her family throughout her life.

"My parents are busy with so many other things that when
I go home to visit, it's like I wasn't there," she said with a look
of disappointment on her face.

Amy shared the memory of when her younger brother was born with medical problems. He received so much attention she felt pushed aside. She felt invisible and insignificant throughout childhood, which continued as a teenager when a boyfriend betrayed her trust and hurt her deeply. Over the years when Amy tried to talk to her parents about her feelings, she said they became defensive and couldn't understand why she felt this way for all they had done for her. This made Amy feel even more rejected.

As an adult, Amy could not understand why she felt a deep sense of insignificance around other people. She remembers being involved in gatherings with friends or coworkers and feeling uncomfortable—like she didn't belong. She felt that even if she did say something, no one would listen anyway. Through counseling, Amy realized she would often pick unhealthy friends who acted similar to her parents, making her feel more insignificant and depressed. Over time Amy began to make healthy choices by distancing herself from the unhealthy people in her life. She was able to release hurt feelings, forgive her parents, build her confidence, and learn to create healthy relationships. Amy was finally able to recognize that she is just as important as anyone else. If you have struggled with your identity or are feeling unimportant, invisible, or that you don't belong, you can declare who you are in Christ.

Preparing Your Heart to Receive What God Has for You

My Father in heaven, thank You for what You have done on the cross for my life, and I ask Your forgiveness for my lack of belief that You created me to be significant.

Heavenly Father, on the basis of Your forgiveness and Your holy Word, I choose to accept that I am significant and receive all that You have declared about me. In Jesus's name, I pray.

Declaring the Truth - I Am Significant

I am a child of the King. I am a co-heir to the King in heaven. Jesus bought and paid for my inheritance from what I have from God and who I am in Jesus Christ. For in Christ I am a new creation; the old things in my life have passed away, and the new and greater things have come. All that I am is from God, who reconciled me to Himself through Christ. Since I am from God, I will recognize between the spirit of truth and the spirit of falsehood. I am significant because I am a child of God living in the Spirit of truth.

In Christ, I choose to forgive and release myself from the curses and lies of past circumstances and people in my life who have created the lies of insignificance. I am forgiven for thinking and believing these lies. In Christ, I am able to bind any evil influence caused by the belief or curse of insignificance over my life. I am free of the past lies and can live in freedom received from what Christ has done on the cross for my sake. I am able to receive my heavenly inheritance of who I am in Christ. And I receive all the heavenly blessings and glory that come with being co-heir with the King.

God showed His love for me by sending His one and only Son into the world that I may live through Him. I am from God, and God is greater than anyone who is in the world. I set my mind on the things above for what God says about me, not on the things that are on earth or what others say about me. In Christ, I am visible, wanted, valuable, significant, accepted, and important. Because what I say and what I do is valuable, significant, and worthy of the King, I am valuable, significant, and worthy for myself and for anyone else that comes into my life. For the love of Christ controls me. Christ died for me so that I no longer need to live for myself but for Him, who died and rose again on my behalf. Whatever I speak, I speak as one who speaks the very words of God. Whenever I serve, I serve with the strength that God supplies so that in all things God may be praised through Jesus Christ. I choose to believe that I am significant in what I do and what I say because of what God says about me and what God does through me.

References

Galatians 4:6-7; 2 Corinthians 5:17-19; Ephesians 1:3, 11; 1 John 4:4, 6; Colossians 3:2; 2 Corinthians 5:14-15; 1 Peter 4:11

I Am Confident

We have boldness and confident access through faith in Him.

Ephesians 3:12

Do you frequently second-guess yourself or question your own ability to succeed, especially with something new? Do you struggle with making decisions, even simple ones? When you struggle with your worth, you can also struggle with your confidence in almost every area of your life. It is important to recognize the potential that is already in you. By declaring words of truth, you can be empowered to believe in yourself.

I remember a man named Wayne said to me, "I've never had confidence in myself. And it's been difficult to make decisions all of my life."

I found out that when he grew up Wayne was rarely allowed to make decisions on his own especially when the adults in his life would correct the decisions he tried to make. So it seemed no matter how hard he tried, the comments from others made him feel that what he did accomplish was not good enough.

What made it worse was when he got married, his wife also made comments to correct him. He found it difficult to break out of his bondage to poor self-confidence.

The negative messages Wayne received as a child became the same messages he began to use toward himself as an adult. And these negative messages continued to keep him locked in the same pattern of life, like a curse against his own confidence. When he was willing to recognize the past hurts as an origin of discouragement, he was then willing to allow God to help him release the hurt and forgive others for what they did. After declaring his confidence, he began to step out in faith and put into practice ideas on his own. For example, Wayne was able to build up his confidence to tell his wife how he felt about her negative comments.

Maybe your confidence level has been low most of your life and you feel that everything you do is a struggle to be good enough. God does not want whatever happened in your past or what is happening in the present to stand in the way of the confidence you can have to accomplish what you can do in the future. Declare your confidence!

Preparing Your Heart to Receive What God Has for You

My Father in heaven, thank You for what You have done on the cross for my life, and I ask Your forgiveness for not believing in what You can do through me. I forgive myself for not believing in myself. Heavenly Father, on the basis of Your forgiveness and Your holy Word, I choose to look to You for my confidence and receive all that You have declared about me. In Jesus's name, I pray.

Declaring the Truth - I Am Confident

I am confident because of who God is through me. My heart will not fear or have struggles in life because I remain confident to see the goodness of the Lord. I will always pray with joy because I am confident knowing that as the heavenly Father began a good work in me, He will carry it on to completion until the day Christ Jesus returns.

In accordance with the eternal purpose, which was carried out in Christ Jesus our Lord, I have boldness and confident access through faith in Him. I will not lose heart at my tribulations that people and circumstances bring my way but stand in the confidence I have through Christ.

In Christ, I am released from any hurtful words or actions from anyone in my life having to do with negative influences over my life. In its place, I receive from heaven the spirit of confidence, encouragement, truth, significance, and blessings that is free for me to obtain. I will not be put to shame in anything, but will stand in the boldness I have in Christ. For Christ will be exalted in me, whether by life or by death, for to me, to live is Christ and to die is gain. My mouth speaks boldly against my enemies because I rejoice in what Christ has done for me. I can speak confidently in whatever I do or say and am confident that the things I do and say in Christ are excellent and profitable for everyone.

I speak the Word of God with freedom and boldness and courage. I am confident that the Lord has delivered me from my past. I will declare something new and it will be established for me and light will shine on my ways. When I am cast down, I will speak with confidence and be saved by God, as I am humble in what I do. I will be delivered when I am innocent, and I will be delivered through the cleanness of my hands. Great is my confidence in Christ, and great is my comfort and overflowing with joy in all my difficulty. I give thanks to God for His loving-kindness and His truth, for God has magnified His Word according to His mighty name. He made me bold with strength in my soul. I have confidence that if I ask anything according to His will, He hears me. I know that God hears me in whatever I ask and know that I have the requests that I have asked from Him.

References

Psalm 27:3; 27:13; Philippians 1:2-7; Ephesians 3:11-13; Philippians 1:19-21; 1 Samuel 2:1; Titus 3:8; Acts 4:31; Job 22:28-30; 2 Corinthians 7:4; Psalm 138:2-3; 1 John 5:14-15

I Am Purposeful

For this very purpose I raised you up, to demonstrate
My power in you...

Romans 9:17

You may be at a time where you don't know what to do with
your life or are struggling to find direction or purpose. Maybe
you had a sudden unplanned job change or you are finishing
a stage of your life and are wondering what God has for you
next. There is often a little discouragement, confusion, and fear
that can accompany the feeling of having a lack of purpose in
your life. These are normal feelings when you don't have something to hold on to, look forward to, or when you have little
knowledge of what to expect. The good news is you are actually
at a better place in your life than you realize. You see, among
the reasons why you feel so lost with little purpose is because
throughout your life you were relying your own way of thinking
and believing. God had been waiting until you were done trying to be in control so you could let Him take control of your
life. God wants you to know how much He wants to meet you
where you are in order to help you get where you need to be.

Maybe you are in a stage in life where your life is changing and you are struggling to find your purpose. That's what happened to me when I made a career change to another job after leaving a hospital where I worked for many years. Although getting accustomed to the new career was a little rough at first, I thought everything was going well. However, after four months on the new job, I was called into my boss's office and given the news that my productivity was not what they were looking for. So without any warning, I was let go on the spot. To say the least, I felt a sense of shock that riveted straight through me. I left feeling numb, completely devastated, wondering what I was going to do to support my wife and new baby son. I felt like an utter failure and blamed myself for changing jobs. I thought I was on the right path in life. But that all changed in a second. Now I was lost and without a true purpose of where God wanted me to be. I began doubting myself and my own abilities as a professional. My overwhelming emotions blocked me from sensing what God wanted for me. I realized this situation was getting the best of me, so I had to do something different. Over the next several months, I attended a men's Bible study, prayed constantly, and received Christian counsel to help me know what to do. Regardless of how I felt, I knew I would find my purpose again, but I realized I had to seek it rather than allow myself to give up.

After waiting upon the Lord and declaring who I was in Christ, I found out my purpose was to return to the career I originally left. I realized I changed careers for the wrong reasons, and without seeking God's guidance and direction, I was lost. Wherever you are in life, as you allow God to be the manager of your purpose, He will direct your path.

Preparing Your Heart to Receive What God Has for You

My Father in heaven, thank You for what You have done on the cross for my life, and I ask Your forgiveness for not believing in what You can do through me. I forgive myself for not believing in You as my guide for the purpose and direction of my life. Heavenly Father, on the basis of Your forgiveness and Your holy Word, I choose to accept my purpose through You and receive all that You have declared about me. In Jesus's name, I pray.

Declaring the Truth - I Am Purposeful

I have been raised up for the very purpose to demonstrate the power of God that is in me so that I may proclaim His holy name throughout the whole earth. I know that God can do all things and no purpose of His can be discouraged. I remember the things God has done in the past, for He is God and there is no one like Him. God can tell me the future before it happens. God's purpose for me will be established, and He will accomplish whatever He wishes. The Lord will set me free for purposes of good. In Christ I am harmonious, sympathetic, brotherly, kindhearted, and humble in spirit—not returning evil for evil or insult for insult, but giving a blessing instead. I am called for the very purpose that I might inherit a blessing in order to give away a blessing to someone else.

I have obtained an inheritance, having been predestined according to His purpose who works all things after the counsel of His will. My hope is in Christ, and I will praise His glory. I will continue to declare what I don't have, and the Holy Spirit will help me with my weakness. As I remain in Christ and

Christ remains in me, I will bear much fruit in what I do. Apart from Christ, I can do nothing. Because I remain in Christ and His words remain in me, all I need to do is ask whatever I desire to the glory of my heavenly Father, and it will be done for me. The Father loves me and gives me His joy and desires that my joy may be full. I am Christ's friend, for everything that Christ learned from His Father, He has made known to me. As I go forth, I will ask the Holy Spirit for direction and wisdom that will come from the Father. Christ chose me and appointed me to do His work so that I might go and bear fruit—fruit that will last—and so that whatever I ask in Christ's name, the Father will give me. God causes all things to work together for my good as I love God and am called according to His purpose. The Holy Spirit helps me pray as He intercedes for me with sounds too deep for words. God is able to make all grace abound in me so that I always have all sufficiency in everything and have abundance for every good deed.

References

Romans 9:17; Job 42:2; Isaiah 46:9-11; Jeremiah 15:11; 1 Peter 3:8-10; Ephesians 1:11; Romans 8:25-26; John 15: 5, 7, 11, 13-15; Romans 8:28; 2 Corinthians 9:8

I Am Attractive
(Inside and Outside)

...Your body is a temple of the Holy Spirit who is in you ... For you have been bought with a price: therefore glorify God in your body.

1 Corinthians 6:19-20

Do you struggle with the way you look or the way you believe others think you look? Is it difficult to go anywhere without spending a great deal of time and effort making yourself look pretty or presentable to the outside world? And when you're ready to go out, do you still wonder if you look good enough?

You may say, "Craig, you don't understand. I'll look terrible if I don't fix myself up."

And my response is, "Where did you get the belief you will look terrible, and what is it about yourself that is *not* attractive? Do you believe people will not like you or you will be rejected? Or do you simply not like something about how you look?"

It is often true that what *you* believe is rarely perceived the same way as those looking at you. Some people would consider spending so much time *fixing up* yourself as a spirit of pride. However, this way of thinking is more likely a deeper sense of inferiority about yourself or a poor self-image that often starts earlier in life. As I mentioned in previous chapters, how we are treated through our life can determine our measurement of value and worth.

During a conversation with Amanda, I commented on how nice she looked with her hairstyle that recently changed. She became quiet as I saw what appeared to be a frown on her face. My questioning look got her attention as I asked, "Is there something wrong with what I said?"

She replied, with some embarrassment, "I guess I have always been uncomfortable with compliments about how I look."

In order to put her at ease, I mentioned how common it is for people to not feel good about themselves.

When I asked Amanda what feelings she had when I gave her a compliment, she said, "I felt uncomfortable, like this heavy weight inside my chest." When we asked the Holy Spirit where Amanda felt this in her past, Amanda remembered she was made fun of as a child because she was overweight. "I hated that time of my life, and I hated how I looked," Amanda said with her eyes beginning to tear up. After emotions of the past were released, Amanda pictured Jesus dancing with her as a little girl. I could almost see the joy bubbling up inside as her face lit up with a big smile. Amanda realized that she is a lovely person because of *who* she is and not from what she believes she is from what others think.

God created you too as a lovely and attractive person who is priceless in His eyes. Being attractive doesn't just mean what you look like on the outside. Your attractiveness has more to do with who you are and what you think about yourself. Stop selling yourself short; believe in all of you. You are attractive because God made you beautiful inside and out.

Preparing Your Heart to Receive What God Has for You

My Father in heaven, thank You for what You have done on the cross for my life, and I ask Your forgiveness for my lack of belief in what You created in me. I forgive myself for the negative way I have viewed myself, and I forgive those who contributed to my negative view. Heavenly Father, on the basis of Your forgiveness and Your holy Word, I choose to accept that I am attractive and receive all that You have declared about me. In Jesus's name, I pray.

Declaring the Truth - I Am Attractive

My heavenly Father formed my inward parts as He wove me in my mother's womb. I give thanks to Him, for I am wonderfully made and wonderful are His works. The Lord fashioned me and made me with His hands. I am precious in God's sight. I am honored and loved by Him. The Lord does not look at my appearance or at the height of my stature; even if I have been rejected by others or have rejected my own appearance, God wants me to know that He does not see me how others see me. Everyone looks at the outward appearance, but the Lord looks at my heart. The Lord is my Redeemer and the one who formed me from the womb. He is the maker of all things who stretched out the heavens. I delight in the fear of the Lord, and

He will not judge by what His eyes see, nor make a decision by what His ears hear.

In Christ, I bind and release myself from any curse or hurtful words from anyone in my life or from the generation before me having to do with my appearance. In its place, I release from heaven into my life the love of God, the spirit of significance, beauty, and His grace, which is free for me to obtain in Jesus's name. For in the sight of God, I am true, I am noble, I am right, I am pure, I am lovely, I am admirable, I am excellent, and I am praiseworthy. God made me beautiful and has also set eternity in my heart, yet no one can fathom what God has done from beginning to end. There is nothing better for me than to be happy and to do good while I live. My beauty does not come from outward appearance, but rather my beauty comes from my inner self, the unfading beauty of a gentle and quiet spirit, which is of great worth in God's sight. My body is a temple of the Holy Spirit, who is in me, whom I have received from God. I do not own my body. I was bought at a price. I present my body as a living and holy sacrifice, acceptable to God, which is my spiritual service of worship. Therefore, I will honor God with my body. I will not judge myself according to my appearance but judge with righteous judgment, for God is righteous and I will look through the eyes of Christ when I see myself.

References:

Psalm 139:13-14; Psalm 119:73; Isaiah 43:4; 1 Samuel 16:7-8; Isaiah 44:24; Isaiah 11:3; 1 Peter 1:3-4; Philippians 4:8; Ecclesiastes 3:11; 1 Corinthians 6:19-20; Romans 12:1; John 7:23-24

I Have the Mind of Christ

…Be transformed by the renewing of your mind, so that you may prove what the will of God is, that which is good and acceptable and perfect.

Romans 12:2

Did you struggle with schoolwork when you were growing up or feel you were not as smart as others? Or maybe other people in your life have spoken critical words toward you, saying you are stupid, dumb, slow, an idiot, etc. These words are very hurtful to your soul and become curses to your life. If you receive a steady diet of negative thoughts and comments in your life, you may begin to believe them. This is especially true when you struggle making decisions or struggle with how smart you believe you are. Your early experiences have the greatest amount of influence because of the important time of learning that takes place during those years.

I remember when my family moved to another state after I completed second grade. As a young child, it was difficult for me to start a new school when entering the third grade. Unfortunately, the school used a different reading and writing system that was not familiar to me. Not only was it a struggle to learn that year, but I felt like a failure when I had to repeat the third grade. Overall, I know my parents and teachers made the right decision for me to repeat a grade, but it was difficult for an eight-year-old to comprehend what was happening. I was still old enough to know there seemed to be something wrong but didn't know how to talk about it, so I did what most children do at that age: I internalized everything as if I had a problem. I had a lot of unanswered questions about school, which only made me question my abilities more. *Why can't I understand the schoolwork?* I would ask myself. *Why am I so stupid? Why am I so dumb?* I just kept these self-judgment thoughts to myself and, from that point on, began to struggle with how smart I was.

In spite of how I felt as a child, there is a happy ending to the story. As I continued in school, I was determined to work hard to overcome my shortcomings. I looked for opportunities and positive relationships to help build my confidence. And the best part is that God has allowed me to use these childhood experiences to help others.

What about you? Do you question your abilities? I am here to tell you God loves you and does not want hurtful comments or actions to make you struggle any longer with what you believe about yourself.

Preparing Your Heart to Receive What God Has for You

> My Father in heaven, thank You for what You have done on the cross for my life, and I ask Your forgiveness for my lack of belief in what You have given me. I forgive myself for not believing in my abilities, and I forgive

those who contributed to my lack of belief. Heavenly Father, on the basis of Your forgiveness and Your holy Word, I choose to accept that I have a mind of Christ and receive all that You have declared about me. In Jesus's name, I pray.

Declaring the Truth - I Have the Mind of Christ

The same God who gives me perseverance and encouragement grants me the same attitude of mind according to Christ Jesus. I have the same attitude of mind with one mind and one voice to glorify the God and Father of our Lord, Jesus Christ. I will conduct myself in a manner worthy of the gospel of Christ and stand firm in one spirit, with one mind striving for the faith of the gospel. I will not be frightened or be alarmed by those who are against me because of what they say or what they do. My stance will be a sign to them that they will be destroyed and I will be saved by God. Regardless of what others do, my salvation is from God. In Christ, I am released from any hurtful words having to do with my mind, my thinking ability, or my intelligence. I receive from heaven the love of God, the spirit of significance, the abundance of intelligence, a clear mind, a peaceful mind, and the spirit of faith, which is free for me to obtain. Christ is able to do exceedingly and abundantly beyond all that I can ask or think according to the power of Christ that works within me.

I prepare my mind to be ready for action, keeping alert in spirit and fixing my hope completely on the grace and blessings that I will have when Jesus Christ is revealed to the world. I am anxious for nothing but consider everything done through prayer. I am grateful as I let my requests be made known to God. The peace of God, which surpasses all comprehension, guards my heart and my mind in Christ Jesus. Whatever is true, whatever is honorable, whatever is right, whatever is pure, whatever is lovely, whatever is of good repute, I will dwell on these things of which are worthy of praise. I do what is right and just, as it is more acceptable to the Lord. I choose to live in the fruit of the Spirit with love, joy, peace, forbearance, kindness, goodness, faithfulness, gentleness, and self-control. Belonging to Christ Jesus, I have crucified the flesh with its passions and desires. I choose to live by the Spirit and keep in step with Him with my mind and heart. I choose not to be conformed to this world but be transformed by the renewing of my mind to show God's will for my life. The things I have learned and received and heard and seen in Christ, I practice, and the God of peace will be with me. In all that I do and say I press on toward the goal to win the prize for which God has called me heavenward in Christ Jesus.

References:

Romans 15:5-6; Philippians 1:27-28; Ephesians 3:20; 1 Peter 1:12-13; Romans 12:2; Philippians 4:6-9; Proverbs 21:3; Galatians 5:22-26; Philippians 3:14

I Am Hopeful

For I know the plans that I have for you," declares the
LORD, "plans for welfare and not for calamity to give you
a future and a hope.

Jeremiah 29:11

Have circumstances in your life become so difficult that you
have lost hope that anything will get better? Have you felt discouraged, fed up, emotionally overwhelmed, or depressed for
so long that you believe you are destined to live this way? Or
maybe you believe you deserve to live this way? You need to
know that none of these statements are true. You are not destined or deserving to live without hope in any circumstance.
You also need to know that how you feel about yourself has an
influence in why you are in these hopeless situations and also
has a bearing on your attitude with how you choose to get out
of them. God does not want you to feel hopeless or lose hope
in any situation.

Anna entered my office stating she was tired of living with a
husband that was physically disrespectful and emotionally abu-
sive. For years she had felt helpless to do anything about her

situation and thought of ending the marriage. Her husband, Ben, had been physically injured for many years with herniated discs in his back that crippled his ability to stand, sit, walk, and lay down without severe pain. Both Ben and Anna felt hopeless to do anything about their situations.

When Anna finally realized she needed to let go of trying fix Ben and their relationship, she was ready to let God take over. So when Anna let go of past emotion that made her feel helpless, she was able to build up the courage to tell Ben her true feelings and her decision that she could not live this way any longer. Hearing this for the first time, Ben realized Anna was serious and became distraught with the potential of losing her. Ben agreed to attend counseling with her and learn what he could do to change.

I remember watching Ben limp down the hall and kneel on the floor of my office because his severe pain made it too difficult to sit in a chair. As we talked about the relationship, I watched him look at Anna and apologize for the way he treated her. Anna had never heard these words before. At that moment, she began to release tears from the deep hurt she had held in for so many years. After more emotional healing and restoration with their relationship, I asked Ben if he wanted prayer for his back. He acknowledged that he had been unsuccessful with fixing his emotional and physical issues. He finally admitted he was ready to let God take over to bring healing to his heart, mind, and body.

I laid my hands on his back, commanding in Jesus's name the pain and injury to leave and physical healing to begin. Ben began to feel intense heat while the pain began to leave. He was amazed that his pain was diminished to nothing. I then asked him to exercise his faith by walking while he accepted and believed in his healing. He walked up and down stairs and did knee bends with no pain. He became overjoyed with how God totally changed his life! When Ben and Anna decided to let go and let God take over their situations, they went from hopelessly discouraged to a hopeful reassurance. Praise God!

Whatever your circumstance, God loves you and wants you to have the assurance of hopeful expectation in every area of your life. Jesus died on the cross to take away your sins, hurts, and diseases. When you accept Jesus in your heart and ask Him to help you release the pain and change your circumstances, you can become more than an overcomer—you can move from a hopeless outlook to a hopeful expectation of what God has for your life.

Preparing Your Heart to Receive What God Has for You

My Father in heaven, thank You for what You have done on the cross for my life. I choose to forgive myself, and I ask Your forgiveness for my lack of hopeful expectations for my life. Heavenly Father, on the basis of Your forgiveness and Your holy Word, I choose to receive Your hope and receive all that You have declared about me. In Jesus's name, I pray.

Declaring the Truth - I Am Hopeful

The plans the Lord declares are to prosper me and not to harm me. The Lord plans to give me hope and a future. I pray to the Lord, and He will listen to me. I will find Him when I seek Him with all my heart. Great is my Lord, abundant in strength, and His understanding is infinite. The Lord rescues me when I am afflicted, and He brings down any evil against me. In Christ, I am able to bind any present or past circumstances that have been considered hopeless and release myself from the curse of hopelessness from the generation before me. I receive from heaven the love of God, the spirit of hope, and the spirit of faith, which is free for me to obtain.

In the Lord I take refuge and will never be ashamed. I am delivered, rescued, and saved. The Lord has given me commandments to save me. He is my constant rock and my fortress that I can continually go to. The Lord has delivered me from the hand of the wicked, from the grasp of those who are evil and cruel, for God is my hope and my confidence from my youth until the end of the age. The eyes of my heart will be enlightened so that I will know what the hope of His calling is, what the riches of the glory of His inheritance in the saints are, and what the surpassing greatness of His power toward me is. These are in accordance with the working of the strength of God's might. I am chosen by God to bear in mind faith, love, and hope in our Lord Jesus Christ. I rejoice in hope, endure in difficulty, and I am devoted in prayer. I choose to share with the Lord's people who are in need and practice kindness. In the same way, the Spirit also helps my weakness. When I do not know how to pray as I should, the Spirit Himself will intercede for me through groanings too deep for words. God searches my heart and knows the mind of the Spirit because the Spirit intercedes for me according with the will of God.

I have peace with God through our Lord Jesus Christ because of my faith and grace in which I now stand. I am grateful in the hope of the glory of God. I exult in my tribulations, knowing that tribulation brings about perseverance, and perseverance produces character, and character produces hope, and hope does not put me to shame because God's love has been poured out into my heart through the Holy Spirit, who has been given to me. I am strong and take courage in my heart because my hope is in the Lord, and I will have hope through perseverance and the encouragement of the Scriptures. I have hopeful expectations for what I do not see and wait eagerly for it because God causes all things to work together for my good according to His purpose.

References

Jeremiah 29:11-12; Psalm 147:5-6; Psalm 71:1-5; Ephesians 1:18-19; 1 Thessalonians 1:2-4; Romans 12:12-13; Romans 8:26; Psalm 31:24; Romans 5:1-5; 15:4; 8:25, 28

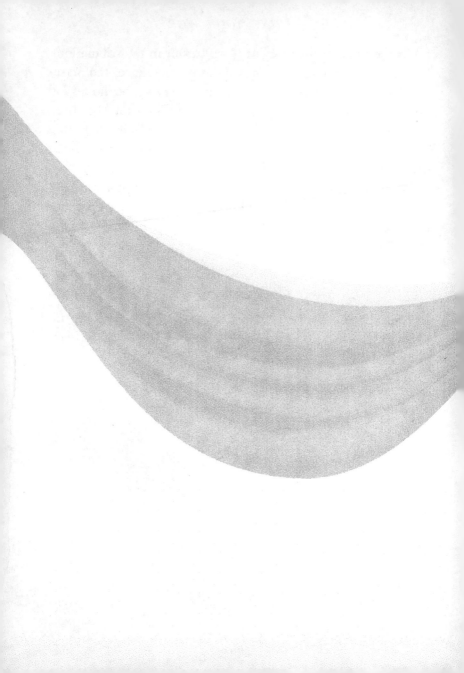

Living in Your Worthiness

What God Wants You to Know

Now that you have declared what God has for your life, you need to learn how to keep living in your worthiness. It is important to live your life different and become mindful of the areas in your daily life that may influence your worth. Take a moment and think about how your worth has been determined from the list below. Next, use the list on page 88 to replace how your worth should be determined in your life. Think about how you can incorporate the list on page 88 into how you think and behave in your daily life.

What my worth should not be determined by:
  What people say about me.
  The church I attend.
  The amount of money I have.
  The things that I own.
  The sins I have committed.
  The accomplishments in my life.
  The way I look or what I say.
  The things I have done.

What my worth should be determined by:

What God says about me.
The God I worship in the church I attend.
How I allow God to use the money I have.
How I allow God to own and use my things.
The forgiveness that I receive for my sins.
How I allow God to use my accomplishments.
How God is seen and heard through me.
What God has done for me.

Affirm Your Own Worth

Research has shown that when you learn something new, it is important to repeat what you have learned in order for the new information to become a part of your daily thoughts and actions. You deserve to hear the truth about yourself and the good things God wants you to know. Celebrate what God says about you by repeating the following declarations every day.

I am loved and lovable.
I am accepted.
I can love others.
I am worthy and significant.
I have an inheritance of blessings from the Lord.
I am blameless.
I am wonderfully made.
I am forgiven and free.
I am victorious.
I am confident.
I am purposeful.

I have the mind of Christ.
I am attractive inside and outside.
I am hopeful of good things to come my way.

Daily Living in Your Worth

In order to live in your worthiness, it is important that you do the following:

1. Eliminate ungodly beliefs and heal any unhealthy emotions that may hold you back from believing in the truth or feeling good physically and emotionally. If necessary, seek professional Christian counseling to assist with this.

2. Guard your heart and mind from the evil and negative influences around you. Beware of how you are treated by others and learn to set boundaries as it is appropriate with people that are negative and dysfunctional in their thoughts and behaviors. Identify your own ungodly thoughts and behaviors that may keep you in bondage to negativity. If you or someone you know speaks a negative thought or word over you, simply say, "In the name of Jesus, I cut off (negative thought/word). It has no place in my life. I replace that with (positive thought/word), in Jesus's name." If necessary seek professional Christian counseling to assist with identifying and changing your lifestyle to eliminate ungodly habits and relationships.

3. Keep yearning and keep declaring the truth by reading the chapters in this book, as well as scriptures in the Bible, to grow in your faith. Declare and simply believe what God says and has for your life.

Other Resources by Craig A Miller
www.insightsfromtheheart.com

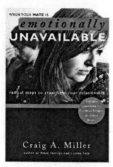

When Your Mate Is Emotionally Unavailable is for those relationships where the lack of emotions, love, and affection continues despite unsuccessful efforts to change the relationship through loving, waiting, complaining, praying, and counseling. This book identifies the characteristics of living with an emotionally unavailable mate, how a person becomes unemotional, why emotional mates love them, the negative impact on the family, ways to bring hope and give encouragement, and practical steps to make radical changes with both the emotional and unemotional mate to rekindle emotion, respect, and affection. Questions after each chapter are available for individual and group study.

Finding Victory: When Healing Doesn't Happen is for those that have prayed for healing with little results. Dr. Randy Clark and Craig Miller teamed up to teach why healing doesn't happen; Why you to lose your healing; How to pray for specific emotional and physical conditions; Changing the atmosphere to believe; Finding power and authority from Christ; What to do when healing is hindered by issues of unworthiness, unbelief, fear, doubt, curses, spiritual warfare, unforgiveness, and more.

For more details, go to www.insightsfromtheheart.com

Other Resources by Craig A Miller
www.insightsfromtheheart.com

THE BOOK—*When Feelings Don't Come Easy* will explain why people struggle to freely express their God-given emotions. You will learn that at the heart of emotional suffering, many physical and emotional ailments, poor self-worth, and dissatisfaction with life is the inability to identify and effectively express feelings. This book provides valuable insights, powerful case examples, inspiring scriptures, and easy-to-learn techniques to understand: why feelings don't come easy, how to identify and express feelings, how to receive more confidence to say what you think, how to stop becoming hurt by what others say, and how to feel better about yourself! Questions after each chapter are available for individual and group study.

DVD—*Better Life Spotlight—Healthy Relationships* is an inspiring and informative ninety-minute DVD taped in front of a live audience at WLMB–TV40 in Toledo, Ohio. Craig will share practical ways to: radically improve how to communicate thoughts and feelings in relationships, increase confidence to say what you think and feel, show loving affection, reduce and handle emotional meltdowns, let go of hurts from others, reduce emotional or phys-  ical stress and suffering, and much more. During a question-and-answer time, you will learn easy steps to teach children how to express healthy emotions and how to help teenagers communicate with you.

For more details, go to www.insightsfromtheheart.com